# ESSENTIAL MANAGERS

London, New York,
Munich, Melbourne, Delhi

**Senior Editor** Peter Jones
**Senior Art Editor** Helen Spencer
**Executive Managing Editor** Adèle Hayward
**Managing Art Editor** Kat Mead
**Art Director** Peter Luff
**Publisher** Stephanie Jackson
**Production Editor** Ben Marcus
**Production Controller** Hema Gohil

Produced for Dorling Kindersley Limited by
**cobaltid**

The Stables, Wood Farm, Deopham Road,
Attleborough, Norfolk NR17 1AJ
www.cobaltid.co.uk

**Editors** Louise Abbott, Kati Dye, Maddy King,
Marek Walisiewicz
**Designers** Darren Bland, Claire Dale, Paul Reid,
Annika Skoog, Lloyd Tilbury, Shane Whiting

First published in 2009 by
Dorling Kindersley Limited
80 Strand, London WC2R 0RL
A Penguin Company

A CIP catalogue record for this book
is available from the British Library.

ISBN 978-1-4053-3545-4

Colour reproduction by
Colourscan, Singapore
Printed and bound in China by
Starlite Development

See our complete catalogue at

**www.dk.com**

# Contents

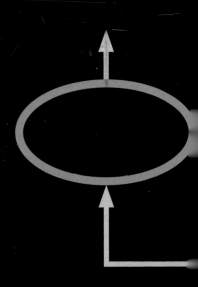

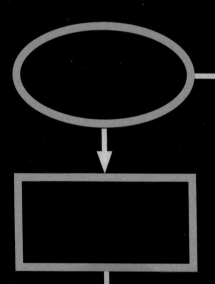

# Introduction

Project management is the skill of moving from ideas to results and, as such, is applicable to every significant initiative we are given or come up with ourselves. Today, individuals, organizations, and nations need project management skills more than ever in a world that values individual and collective initiative above just about any other attribute.

*Project Management* outlines a range of practical understandings and skills that will make your projects both successful and satisfying. It will provide you with common-sense solutions to the project management issues you will face as you plan and implement a project, and the tools, tips, and techniques it contains are intended to help you achieve consistent success using minimum resources. The book is written for those taking their first steps in project management, but also offers helpful reminders to those with more experience.

In the final analysis, your success as a project manager is down to you; it will depend on your ability to make your vision of "what can be" more influential in your own and other people's thinking and actions than the reality of "what currently is". If the following pages guide, challenge, and energize you in this quest they will have fulfilled their purpose.

# Chapter 1

# Thinking "project"

Projects are the mechanism by which organizations and individuals change and adapt to take advantage of new opportunities or counter threats. In a world in which business competitiveness is based on a search for new products and ways to do things, every individual can improve their prospects by always thinking: "Where is the project in my current situation?"

# What is a project?

A project is a piece of work that is designed to bring about an agreed beneficial change within a fixed timeframe using specified resources. Projects usually require the coordinated activity of a number of people to achieve that outcome, and often incorporate an element of risk.

## What makes a task a project?

Projects are the way in which human creativity is most effectively harnessed to achieve tangible, lasting results. In the past they may have been called something different, but building a pyramid, painting a ceiling, or founding a nation all required vision, planning, and coordinated effort – the essential features of what we now call a project. In practical terms, just about any initiative or piece of work that is too large or unfamiliar to be completed successfully without some measure of preparation and planning can, and usually should, be approached as a project.

# Defining a project

At its simplest level, a project is a "one-off" scope of work defined by three parameters – time, cost, and quality. In other words, it is the means by which a particular result is delivered using specified resources within a set timeframe.

For most projects, one of these three parameters is "fixed" (i.e. should not or cannot change), but there is flexibility in at least one of the other two. Where the quality of the product is fixed (bringing a new drug to market, for example), costs have a tendency to rise and deadlines to slip if work is more extensive or complex than was first envisaged. Where the deadline is fixed (as for a tender deadline or a business conference), people either throw more resources at the project to make sure that it is ready on time, or they cull desirable but non-essential features in order to deliver the essential elements of quality within the timeframe available.

## Achieving change

Some projects are highly visible – large and prestigious building projects, for example – while for others, no-one except those directly involved has any understanding of, or interest in, what they will deliver.

Whatever the size and nature of a project, the principal aim is always to bring about a change that is viewed as beneficial by the person or people sponsoring it.

## CASE STUDY

### Setting the standard

When Tim Smit pitched the idea of creating a science-based visitor attraction showcasing 100,000 plants from around the world in a disused clay pit in South West England, few would have expected the Eden Project to have become the icon it is today. Despite the technological challenges of creating the world's largest greenhouses – two giant transparent domes – the main construction phase was complete by March 2001. Since then, it has been visited by more than 10 million people at a rate of over one million a year, and has brought over £850m to the local economy. Just as importantly to Smit, Eden is now a significant contributor to the global debate on sustainable development and environmental issues. As with any high-profile project, commentators offer a variety of explanations for its success: technology made the original design and spectacular scale possible, but Smit's vision, inspirational leadership, and refusal to compromise on quality were undoubtedly central.

# The project sequence

The lifecycle of any project consists of six main phases: initiation, definition, planning, control, implementation, and review. At whichever point you, as project manager, enter the project's life, be sure to acquaint yourself as fully as possible with any preceding phases you have missed.

**TIP**

**FOCUS ON DEFINITION**

Fully explore the "whats" and "whys" of the project before you start to make practical plans – this will help you avoid the need for costly revisions in later phases.

## Defining project phases

The initiation and definition phases involve using tools and approaches to identify the situation to be addressed, the desired end result, and the core team responsible for making it happen. Once these are established, the planning phase focuses on the detail of what has to be produced and how this can be done most effectively with minimum risk. While planning continues throughout the project, there is generally a point at which significant resources are committed, and the control phase sees work begin.

The schedules and budgets that you established while planning will allow you to track progress and make adjustments as needed. As the control phase nears completion, focus switches to preparation for

## The six phases of a project:

**INITIATION**
Identifying the problem to be solved or opportunity to be exploited.

**DEFINITION**
Refining your understanding of what you want to achieve, by when, and with what resources.

**PLANNING**
Deciding in detail how to achieve the objective – timescales, resources, responsibilities, and communications.

the moment when the results will "go live". While you should have been considering the needs and expectations of end users at every stage, your primary focus during this implementation phase should be taking steps to ensure that they react positively to the change your project has brought about. Plan your review stage around pre-defined criteria by which the project's success can be measured. These can then be used to declare it complete before moving into a phase where resources are reallocated and lessons learnt.

## Maintaining flexibility

While in theory the phases provide a logical sequence, in practice they often overlap, so you need to adopt a rolling process of continuous review during the definition, planning, and control phases. For example, you may need to modify the initial scope* of a project to fit with what proves to be possible once you have produced a first draft of the plan. Similarly, experience gained from work early in the project may lead you to identify flawed assumptions about the duration and complexity of tasks, leading to a re-evaluation of timescales, budgets, and other resources.

**\*Scope** — *a description of the desired end result of a project. For clarity, it often includes reference to the context in which the end result will be delivered, and who the end user will be.*

**CONTROL**
Doing the work, monitoring progress, and adjusting the plan according to need.

**IMPLEMENTATION**
Passing what you have created over to those who will be using it, and helping them to adjust to any changes.

**REVIEW**
Assessing the outcome and looking back to see if there is anything you could have done differently or better.

# Defining the team

Role clarity is essential if you are to deliver a successful project. As every project is a new and often unique scope of work, and project teams are often built from scratch, it is vital that each stakeholder* in your project is clear about exactly what their role entails and what they will be expected to deliver.

## Understanding key roles

Every project is different, but there are a number of key roles that apply to most projects (see right). The relationship between these roles is functional rather than hierarchical. Although by the nature of the role the sponsor will usually be the most senior member of the project team – and will certainly be more senior than the manager – little else can be assumed about the relative seniority of other team members. Technical specialists, in particular, frequently have skills based on years of experience and are often "senior" to the project manager.

## Knowing your team

Your project team will generally be made up of people from your organization and contractors – referred to as internal and external team respectively. Clearly these are key stakeholders in the success of your project, so as project manager you must make their motivation and focus a priority. This may take some skill and effort: team members frequently have other work to juggle. In addition, they will be influenced by a second ring of stakeholders over whom you have no direct control (or of whom you have no knowledge), such as their line managers, colleagues, clients, and suppliers.

**\*Stakeholder** — *anyone who has influence over, or interest in, the process or outcome of a project.*

**TIP**

**BEWARE THE BUYER**

Buyers often wield significant power where a project has been procured. Those that also act as the client can sometimes have an adversarial relationship with the project. Handle such clients carefully, using the sponsor where necessary.

# Key project roles

## SPONSOR
The person who owns the resources needed for success and on whose authority the project takes place.

## MANAGER
Has day-to-day executive responsibility for the project. Manager and sponsor must be in complete agreement about what constitutes success with respect to time, cost, and quality.

## TECHNICAL SPECIALISTS
In many projects, success depends on the input of a small number of people with expert skills, high levels of access, or personal decision-making authority.

## CLIENT (OR SENIOR USER)
Coordinates or represents the interests of the end-user group. If there are multiple end-user groups with differing views, there may be a number of clients.

## BUYER
Buyers procure or commission projects on behalf of end users, and are judged primarily on their ability to source suppliers and negotiate competitive rates on contracts.

## QUALITY ASSURANCE
In larger projects, a team may be assigned to ensure that all prescribed methodologies are carried out properly. (In smaller projects, the sponsor should do this.)

## END USERS
End users are often represented by the client, but there are key moments in most projects when it is helpful to communicate directly with this group.

# Being project manager

As a project manager, you will be the central hub around which your project team is formed. Much of your success will depend on your ability to make the project something others want to be involved in or, at the very least, do not want to oppose.

## Owning the project

Whether you have been delegated the role of project manager, or you sold an idea upwards to someone capable of sponsoring it, you are likely to have demonstrated personal and managerial competence and commitment to the change under consideration.

"Competence" and "commitment" are the sorts of solid but colourless words often found in management books; however, the last thing a project manager can afford to be is colourless. Indeed, the very best project managers are a paradoxical combination of "larger than life" – self-confident, decisive, creative, and engaging; and self-effacing – down to earth, hands on, and keen to learn from other members of their team and promote their contributions.

## Selling the idea

To be fully convincing as a project manager, you must first be convinced of the value of the initiative under consideration yourself. If you do not believe the results are attainable, or are lukewarm about their value, you are unlikely to make the sacrifices or identify the creative solutions required when the going gets tough – as it almost invariably will at some point. Furthermore, you must be able to communicate your enthusiasm to others and have the confidence to stand up to opposition both inside and outside the

# ✔ CHECKLIST **AM I READY TO MANAGE THIS PROJECT?**

| | YES | NO |
|---|---|---|
| • Do I have a clear idea of who the end users are in my project and what the world looks like through their eyes? | ☐ | ☐ |
| • Do I understand what is required of this project and why? | ☐ | ☐ |
| • Do I care about the outcome enough to make personal sacrifices to achieve it? | ☐ | ☐ |
| • Am I confident I can deliver it given the constraints of cost and time? | ☐ | ☐ |
| • Am I prepared to take risks and back my own judgement where necessary? | ☐ | ☐ |

project team. Conversely, you must be a good listener – able to sift through the opinions of others and take on their ideas whenever they improve the quality of outcome or the likelihood of success.

# Taking on responsibility

To be an effective project manager, you must have a balance of task- and people-related skills. While your ultimate aim is to deliver a result, success comes from building diverse individuals into a strong team and motivating them to produce quality results within the requisite timeframes. Often, you will achieve this through personal determination, creativity, and powers of persuasion. At a deeper level, you also need the moral courage and integrity to treat every member of the team the same, irrespective of their seniority and personality. You also need excellent time management and personal organization, so that you can think beyond immediate distractions or crises to provide proactive leadership to other members of the team. While it is important to have at least some understanding of the technical aspects of the project, your management role is to provide the decision-making, planning, and leadership skills outlined in this book.

**TIP**

**PLAY DEVIL'S ADVOCATE**

Anticipate opposition by thinking through possible criticisms of your project and coming up with effective counter-arguments so that you are well prepared to tackle negative views.

# Working with your sponsor

The relationship between the project manager and the sponsor is the foundation upon which the whole project is built. Both must have the same understanding of what constitutes success and must have established a relationship of trust that enables each to share issues and concerns with the other as soon as they crop up.

**TIP**

**AVOID SURPRISES**
Never try to hide things that have gone wrong from your sponsor – even if this means admitting a serious mistake on your part.

## Engaging the sponsor

Your sponsor should be the individual (rather than the group, team, or committee) who owns the resources required to make the project successful and will act as the final arbiter of success. This will be based partly on hierarchical seniority and partly on personal authority. Effective sponsorship is one of the key determinants of your success, so a wise project manager invests time and effort, firstly in selecting the right person – if you have a choice; secondly in forging the right relationship; and thirdly in providing the sponsor with the information and arguments he or she needs to defend or champion the project as necessary.

## IN FOCUS... CHOOSING YOUR OWN PROJECT SPONSOR

If you are in a position to choose your sponsor, your goal should be to achieve just the right balance between authority and accessibility. While it is generally helpful to have as senior a sponsor as possible, you also need someone for whom the project is significant enough to command their active interest. A sponsor who keeps up to date with your progress and is aware of potential or actual issues will be well placed to make decisions or help you overcome any opposition or obstacle to the project without the need for extensive briefing. You need to be able to consult your sponsor quickly when things go wrong and feel comfortable that you are more than just one commitment among many.

# Meeting your sponsor

Your first meeting with the sponsor of your project is a key moment of influence. This meeting should not be just about the detail of the project, but must also establish how you and the sponsor will work together to make the project succeed. Give high priority to agreeing communication channels and escalation procedures – how and when to involve the sponsor when things go wrong. In larger projects, key team members such as a senior user or technical specialist may also be invited to attend this meeting.

# Identifying poor sponsorship

Beware the sponsor who cancels or postpones your meetings at short notice, or who fails to get your project on to the agenda of key decision-making meetings. Quickness to apportion blame, or to get unnecessarily embroiled in detail, are other indications that your sponsor has become detached from the aims and progress of your project. Think very carefully about what you should do and who you might speak to if your sponsor's lack of engagement starts to threaten the success of your project.

## HOW TO... FORGE A GOOD SPONSOR–MANAGER RELATIONSHIP

Be clear on your own role: this will give the sponsor confidence that you are the right person for the job.

↓

Express clear expectations of them to ensure you set a worthwhile "contract" upon which to build your relationship.

↓

Take time to establish personal rapport with the sponsor.

↓

Ask about other projects they have sponsored and project managers they have worked with, to establish their style of working and likes and dislikes.

↓

Use examples and scenarios to agree how you should interact when things go wrong.

↓

Find out from them what information they require, when or how frequently they need it, and what format they would like it in.

# Documenting progress

Standard documents and agreed circulation and sign-off procedures increase the efficiency of project teams and improve communication, particularly between sponsor and manager. If your organization does not yet have a standard set of project documents, you can enhance your reputation considerably by producing your own.

**TIP**

**INVEST TIME EARLY ON**
It is often difficult to find the time in a busy schedule to develop and manage project paperwork, but a little time spent considering documentation early on will get your project off on the right foot.

## Designing documentation

Having a suite of carefully designed project documents allows information to be carried over from one project milestone to the next – or even from project to project – and helps occasional stakeholders find information quickly within a particular document. Simple formats work best, and should incorporate a cover sheet identifying the document, the project to which it refers, and the key stakeholders involved. Never underestimate presentation: people are quick to judge based on first impressions, and if your paperwork looks professional, they will treat you as such unless you subsequently prove otherwise.

## Using document sign-offs

The practice of physically signing off documents is a very useful way to get people to take a project seriously. However, any decision about whether to use it needs to be sensitive to the culture of your organization: if people are generally good at engaging with projects and delivering on promises, then asking for signatures may be seen as unnecessarily aggressive. If this is not the case and a firmer line is required, implementing a policy of signing off documents is most easily achieved if you employ it from the start, with all document formats having space for signatures.

# Key project documents

Each of the six phases of your project requires different documentation to record important details. Depending on the size and nature of your project, these may include:

## 01

### INITIATION PHASE
- **Mandate:** agreement of the need for the project and its aims.
- **Brief:** a description of the issue to be resolved or the opportunity to be exploited.

## 02

### DEFINITION PHASE
- **Project Initiation Document (PID):** defines what the project must deliver and why.
- **Business case:** the financial figures behind the opportunity.
- **Risk log:** a record of all risks and approaches to resolution.

## 03

### PLANNING PHASE
- **Schedule and resource plans:** the plan in detail, including completion dates and resource requirements.
- **Quality plan:** what processes will be monitored, and how.

## 04

### CONTROL PHASE
- **Changes to scope:** agreed modifications to the original brief.
- **Milestone reviews:** progress against schedule and budget.
- **Quality reviews:** confirmation that processes are being followed.

## 05

### IMPLEMENTATION PHASE
- **User Acceptance Test (UAT):** reports and sign-offs from end users at all levels.
- **Implementation schedule:** the plan for how the project will be handed over to end users.

## 06

### REVIEW PHASE
- **Post-implementation review:** assesses what the project has delivered.
- **Lessons learnt review:** how things could have been done better.

# Chapter 2

# Setting up a project

A successful project depends on clear thinking in the preparatory stages. The initiation and definition phases of the project management process build on each other to establish precisely what the project is expected to deliver to the end users, while the planning phase sets out how this is to be achieved.

# Initiating the project

The aim of the initiation phase is to set out the reasons for a project and the context in which it will run. As project manager your aim in this phase is to secure the briefing, backing, and resources you need from your sponsor to begin a detailed evaluation of the work to be undertaken.

## Agreeing the brief

The first step in the initiation phase is to establish that both you and your sponsor view success in the same terms – both the result to be achieved and the way you will work together to achieve it. Based on these discussions the project mandate and brief can be drawn up. These should document, respectively, the business opportunity or issue to be addressed, and some outline thoughts on how this might best be done. The initiation phase should end with the sponsor signing off the brief and allocating resources that allow you to move into the definition and planning phases of your project.

# Getting the right support

The type of support you need from your sponsor during this phase will to a degree be dependent on where the idea for the project came from.

• **Top-down initiation** In most organizations, targets for future development and plans for a variety of initiatives become projects undertaken by operational managers. In this kind of "top-down" initiation, the sponsor delegates the execution of the project to you. This is a critical point for you: do not let nerves or excitement cloud your judgement of what you need at this stage. You can expect strong support from above, but need to secure a very clear brief of what is expected of the project.

• **Bottom-up initiation** Not all the best ideas come from those at the top of an organization; those closest to the customer may be first to spot commercial opportunities. Successful projects initiated from the "bottom up", by people who end up managing them, indicate a very healthy corporate culture. It shows that those at more junior levels are having initiative rewarded with real responsibility – and this represents an opportunity that should be seized. Your advantage in this case is that you will be highly motivated, with a very clear idea of what you want to achieve and how this could be made possible. Your priority is to obtain solid support from a sponsor who is fully behind the project so that you can go on to deliver results that justify his or her confidence in you.

## IN FOCUS...
## PITCHING YOUR OWN PROJECT

If you identify an opportunity requiring more resources than you personally can muster, your first step should be to target a suitable sponsor and pitch your idea. Your presentation should identify the size of the opportunity and be supported by hard evidence. Think about the questions your sponsor might ask. Prepare well: there are unknowns and risks in any project, so your sponsor's decision will be based as much on your credibility as the strength of the idea. Even if you do not get sponsorship for this idea, you can enhance your prospects of getting future projects sponsored if you have put a well-argued case forward.

# Building a project team

One of the most important functions of the project manager is to build and maintain the "team dynamic". By giving your project a strong and positive identity, and making the team a rewarding environment in which to work, you increase the likelihood that people will give you that "extra 10 per cent" that dramatically increases the quality of their contribution and reduces the amount of effort it takes to manage them.

## Putting a team together

An effective project manager builds a team with a strong sense of identity. This is often more challenging in a small team than in one with a higher profile and fully dedicated team members. Start by taking time to select the right people, with input from the sponsor. Base your decisions on availability and relevant skills/knowledge/contacts, but also take personality "fit" and motivation into account. Stakeholder analysis (described overleaf) can be a useful tool for assessing potential candidates and finding the best way to manage them. Make a personal approach to each person selected and request their participation. Don't beg; simply explain why you have selected them and the benefits they can expect for being involved.

### ✔ CHECKLIST CREATING A STRONG TEAM

| | YES | NO |
|---|---|---|
| • Do my team know one another? | ☐ | ☐ |
| • Do they respect one another? | ☐ | ☐ |
| • Do they know how their roles fit together? | ☐ | ☐ |
| • Have they agreed the standards to which they will hold one another accountable? | ☐ | ☐ |
| • Do they acknowledge my role as project manager? | ☐ | ☐ |

# Getting started

Hold an initial meeting with all project team members. It is helpful to have the sponsor present for a proportion of a "kick-off" meeting, but you will enhance your authority as the project manager if you are the one to arrange and chair the meeting. (If you do not have the authority to do this, you may struggle to manage the group through the rest of the project.)

Discuss team roles and ground rules for your project before getting into the detail of the task to be undertaken. People appreciate being asked about their experience of project teamwork, whether there is anything they particularly like or dislike, and what their hopes and concerns are. Talk with the group about how project decisions (particularly in relation to deadlines) will be made; how the team will acknowledge success; what to do if people fail to deliver; and how conflicts will be resolved.

# Developing identity

A strong team is built on a strong identity. Give your project a name, but beware of choosing anything too clever – the best names are generally low key, with positive connotations, offering a useful shorthand reference for the project. Create a team location, be it a building, room, desk, or notice board, or a virtual location on the intranet or web. Make it somewhere that information can be displayed and progress checked, and give people reasons to frequent it.

Members of your team will take greater "ownership" of your project if they feel as if they are an important part of it. Involve them in production of the work schedule, risk analysis, and problem solving. Establish "soft" success criteria, relating to teamwork, morale, personal behaviour, and learning, in addition to the hard criteria set out in your project definition.

# Analyzing stakeholders

The various stakeholders in your project – from the sponsor to each individual internal team member – all view it from very different perspectives. Analysis of each stakeholder's attitude towards your project, and their degree of influence within it, can be a useful part of the process by which a team is put together and managed.

## Identifying key players

All projects have multiple stakeholders. Some will be more important than others, either because of their involvement in delivering elements of the work, or because they are influential in the environment where the work is being produced or will be deployed.

Stakeholder analysis allows you to identify the most important people in your project and decide where to invest time and resources. It should lead to a communication plan aimed initially at canvassing opinion and then providing the right people with timely information throughout the project's lifecycle.

**GET PROOF**
Don't ascribe the highest level of attitude towards the project – being wholly committed – to a stakeholder unless you find positive proof in their words and actions that they are both intellectually and emotionally committed.

## Performing the analysis

Consider every stakeholder in your project in relation to two scales – influence and attitude. Rate each person or group according to their influence within the project, and whether they can be influenced by you as the project manager. Next, rate them on their attitude towards the project. Use the matrix on the facing page to mark the desired and actual position of stakeholders: draw a circle on the grid where you want them to be and a cross where they currently are. Where circles and crosses are co-located consider what you need to do to maintain their position; where they are separate consider what you need to do to improve the situation.

# Influencing stakeholders

As a general rule, you are unlikely to be able to move strongly negative stakeholders to the positive side, but it may be possible to neutralize their opposition. Where there is opposition from an especially powerful stakeholder or group of stakeholders, steps may have to be taken to reduce their influence or the project may have to be abandoned.

Your relationship with the sponsor, and his or her position in your organization, may be very helpful. You need to have the confidence to address senior or challenging stakeholders directly, but also the wisdom to know when this may be counterproductive and a situation is better addressed by involving the sponsor.

## STAKEHOLDER ANALYSIS MATRIX

| INFLUENCE WITHIN THE PROJECT | | Wholly committed | Generally positive | Neutral | Generally opposed | Actively opposed |
|---|---|---|---|---|---|---|
| Significant influence; cannot always be influenced by you | | | | | | |
| Marginal influence; cannot always be influenced by you | | ◯ ◀— X | | Technical specialist | | |
| Influence equal to you | | | | ⊗ Quality assurance manager | | |
| Significant influence; can be influenced by you | | | ◯ ◀———————— | | X | Internal team member |
| Marginal influence; can be influenced by you | | | | | | |

**ATTITUDE TOWARDS THE PROJECT**

# Defining the details

Before committing significant resources, you must have agreement on what your project should produce, by when, and using what resources. While the brief should have identified the rationale and broad strategy behind a project, the next step is to define the scope of the project – precisely what will be handed over to the end users on completion.

## Asking for input

In broad terms, defining the scope of your project is done by asking the right people the right questions in the right way, and recording your findings clearly. Consider the most important players in your project, identified in your stakeholder analysis: which of these have key roles in defining what the project must deliver? Time invested discussing the project brief with stakeholders, particularly the client and end users, is rarely wasted. The views of the sponsor are a good starting point – if your project required an initiation phase, you will have already obtained these from the mandate and the brief. Clients and end users should have significant input into the scope of your project, but also consider those with whom they interact, such as anyone who manages the end users or who will support them in areas relating to your project after implementation. It may also be helpful to speak to anyone who will be responsible for maintaining the product, capability, or facility that your project will deliver.

**What?**
- **What is the problem to be fixed?**
- **What would be the impact of not fixing it?**
- **What exactly is the result required?**
- **What has been tried before?**

**Why?**
- **Why is this result required?**
- **Why doesn't it exist already?**

# Gathering information

Focused and well-structured conversations not only deliver useful information from stakeholders, but can also build your credibility with the client. Generally speaking, it is best to have these discussions face-to-face, as this allows you to assess each person's understanding of, and commitment to, the project. Although your primary purpose is to uncover the information you need to create a clear scope, in-depth questioning often exposes hitherto unexplored aspects of people's work to scrutiny. This can sometimes be resented, so tread carefully, but be courageous enough to continue lines of questioning that are uncovering useful information.

**How?**
- How will it be used?
- How long will it be in service for?

**Where?**
- Where will it be used? (Physically, and in what context?)
- Where is this in our list of priorities?

Asking the right questions to define the scope

**Who?**
- Who are the end users?
- Who will support it?
- Who will manage it?

**When?**
- When will it be used?

# IN FOCUS... THE FIVE WHYS

A simple but surprisingly powerful technique for establishing the link between a project and your organization's key strategic objectives is to ask the client why they want what the project delivers. Insist that they answer this question beginning with the words "in order to". Then take the answer they give and ask them why

*that* is important; again, insist on "in order to". Repeat this process for as many times as it takes to connect your project to your organization's main business strategy. As a rule of thumb, if the sequence of questioning does not lead to one of your organization's strategic goals within five steps, then the project may not be worth pursuing.

**TIP**

**ASK "GREAT QUESTIONS"**

Think carefully about the questions you ask your client. If you can get him or her to say "That's a great question!" you will have helped them uncover a new perspective, and transformed your status from supplier to partner.

# Understanding your client

Your first aim should be to establish how well your client understands the situation surrounding your project and the benefit they expect it to deliver. Inexperienced project managers sometimes make the mistake of trying to zero in too quickly on what the client sees as the essential and desirable features of the end product. In cases where the client does not know what they want, avoid asking direct questions about the scope, as this is likely to confuse and could lead to frustration, embarrassment, and conflict – not the ideal start to a relationship that should become a central axis of the project team.

**TIP**

**CREATE A BOTTOM LINE**

Set a "Fit for Purpose Baseline" – the minimum that your project can deliver and still be deemed a success.

# Prioritizing features

In most projects, as you go through the definition process you will identify a number of features required of the end result. Some will be essential, while others are "nice to have". In order to highlight where clashes exist, take each feature in turn and create designs based on that alone; then consider the results with the client and develop a definition that delivers the perfect mix of features to the end user.

# Adding creativity

As part of the definition phase of your project, it is always worth taking a moment to think how it could be transformed from delivering a "fit for purpose" solution to being a project that catches the eye for creativity and elegance. This need not take much time; the main thing is to suspend judgement on ideas and have some fun. Then change your mindset and assess what additional perspectives your creative musings have uncovered. Try to identify more than one option – even when there is an obvious solution. Take time to consider at least three possible approaches (one of these might be "do nothing"). Your aim should be to find one way to make your project exciting and different for your end users or for your team.

# Recording the scope

The investigations you undertake during the definition phase are to enable you to generate a detailed Project Information Document (PID). This is an expansion of the brief, incorporating all the additional information you have gathered from discussions with stakeholders. The PID is the document on which the sponsor will make a decision on whether to commit significant resources to the project. Once signed off, it becomes a binding agreement between the sponsor, the project manager, and the client, so its format and content are of paramount importance. The information in the PID needs to be easily accessible, so don't include more than is necessary for the size and complexity of your project.

## ✔ CHECKLIST **UNDERSTANDING THE SCOPE OF YOUR PROJECT**

|  | YES | NO |
|---|---|---|
| • Do you have a clear idea of the objective of your project – what it is intended to achieve? | ☐ | ☐ |
| • Do you know why this is important? | ☐ | ☐ |
| • Do you know how and when it will be achieved? | ☐ | ☐ |
| • Have you determined who will be involved? | ☐ | ☐ |
| • Have you identified the deliverables for your project? | ☐ | ☐ |
| • Have you obtained enough information to allow your sponsor to make a decision on whether to proceed? | ☐ | ☐ |

# Developing a business case

Every project will represent an investment in time, effort, and resources, so a key question to address during the definition phase is: "Is this project worth it?" The business case for a project weighs up two factors: the cost of undertaking the project and the benefits it is likely to deliver.

## Weighing up costs

When assessing the potential costs of your project, make sure you only take future costs into account – past expenditure is irrelevant in deciding whether to take the project forward. Only include incremental costs in your assessment: those that change as a result of the project being undertaken. For example, if your project requires that you hire two extra staff but is running from company offices, the additional staff costs should be included but the accommodation costs should not.

## GETTING THE BUSINESS CASE RIGHT

| FAST TRACK | OFF TRACK |
|---|---|
| Using the sponsor's financial advisors to put together your business case | Basing your business case on your own gut feelings and untested assumptions |
| Setting a notional hourly rate for work done by internal team members, especially technical specialists | Considering internal team costs a "free" resource when additional or unplanned work has to be done |
| Including contingency funds in your cost assessment, to allow for unexpected outlays | Deciding to ignore potential risks and take the chance that nothing will go wrong |

Your assessment should include any costs relating to the involvement of your internal team – often known as an invisible cost as no money changes hands – and out-of-pocket costs, which are those that will be paid outside your organization, such as the cost of materials or sub-contracted services.

## Assessing benefits

While it is often easy to identify the "change" your project will deliver, it may be more difficult to quantify the nature, scale, and timing of the benefit. As a rule, the benefits from a project should be aligned with at least one of the organization's strategic goals (such as increasing revenue or reducing costs, for example) if it is to proceed. Consider also the point at which the benefits can be expected. In some cases, a smaller return earlier is preferable to a larger one that will take longer to come in. Projected benefits can rarely be guaranteed and so any complete cost/benefit analysis should contain an assessment of what could go wrong and the effect of this on the overall outcome. While your aim should be to put a percentage figure on the likelihood for the project delivering the intended benefit, this is always a judgement based on incomplete information. In the end it is your sponsor's job to make the decision, but it must be based on accurate information provided by you.

**TIP**

**KNOW YOUR STUFF**

Work with experts to put your business case together, but make sure you understand the basis on which they have done this well enough to form a view on what they have produced.

# Managing risk

Projects, by their nature, are risky, so it could therefore be argued that your key role as a project manager is to identify, plan for, and manage risk. Risk analysis is undertaken in the definition phase, but should be followed by a continuous cycle of management and analysis throughout the control and implementation phases of your project.

## Planning for risk

Initial identification of risk often takes the form of a Risk Workshop – a group of people getting together with the express intention of identifying and evaluating all the risks in a particular project or phase. From that point on every review meeting should contain an agenda item on "open" or "live" risks. As a project manager, the risks you should be most concerned with are those that will have an impact on one of the three project parameters (time, cost, or quality).

**PREVENT**
**Terminate the risk by doing things differently. This is not always a realistic possibility.**

Risks need to be evaluated with respect to two criteria: probability (how likely they are to happen) and impact (how serious it would be if they do). Most tasks in your project will contain some element of risk, so you will need to set a threshold at which you are going to begin to plan. For tasks that carry a risk that is above your threshold for probability and impact, identify a response in advance, and monitor progress towards completion more carefully than usual.

In all but the smallest projects, risks should be recorded in a risk log. This document describes each risk, its impact and probability, and countermeasures to deal with it. It can also include the proximity of the risk (when it will need active management) and any early indicators that the probability of the risk has changed. The contents of the risk log should be reviewed throughout the lifecycle of the project.

## PLAN CONTINGENCY

Have a Plan B that will achieve the same result by a different route and leave future plans intact.

## Dealing with risk

These are the five ways of dealing with risk, as outlined in the internationally recognized project management standard PRINCE2.

## REDUCE

Take action to reduce either the likelihood or impact of the risk.

# Planning the project

The production of an accurate and detailed plan is one of the project manager's most important responsibilities. However, do not make the mistake of thinking you should do it on your own. By involving the team in the planning process you increase their understanding of what has to be done and generally gain an extra level of commitment to deadlines.

## Developing a project plan

The following ten-step Team Planning technique uses sticky notes and a flip chart to produce a project plan. By following the process outlined, you will produce a robust and accurate project plan and maximize buy-in from those who will be instrumental in delivering it. Do the first four steps in this process on your own, getting the team involved once you have some raw material for them to work on. This reduces the cost of planning and makes briefing easier as you have something to show them.

**PROJECT OBJECTIVE**

BY: (DATE)

DELIVER: (PRODUCT)

TO: (CLIENT/END USER)

IN ORDER TO: (BENEFIT)

**1 Restate the objective** Start by reducing the objective of your project – defined in the initiation and definition process – into a single statement of intent that fits on one large sticky note (see left).

**PRODUCT**
e.g. MANUALS
PRINTED

**2 Brainstorm the products** The products of a plan are the building blocks that, when added together, deliver that project's end result. Brainstorm between five and 15 products for your project on separate sticky notes, and place them in roughly chronological order down the short side of a piece of A1 flip chart paper.

**3** **Brainstorm the tasks** Tasks are activities or actions undertaken by individuals or groups that normally require their presence or participation for the whole duration. Take a pack of sticky notes in a different colour to the one you used to set out the products. Brainstorm the tasks that need to be done by you and other people to deliver each of the products, writing one task on to one sticky note. Draw two fields on the bottom half of the sticky note, so that you can add additional information later.

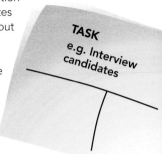

TASK
e.g. Interview candidates

**4** **Place the tasks in order** Place the tasks in roughly chronological order across the page, keeping them in line with the product to which they are connected. Where tasks can be done simultaneously, place them below one another, and where they depend on one another or on using the same resources, place them sequentially. Involve the rest of the delivery team in adding to and refining this skeleton plan.

TIP

**USE COLOUR**
Choose a different colour of sticky note for the objective, the products, and the tasks of your project (here, orange, pink, and yellow, respectively) to give at-a-glance clarity to your plan.

**5** **Confirm the tasks** Step back and look at the logic flow of your plan. Involve the implementation team in this step – it can be a useful "reality check" on your logic. When people identify modifications to your plan, listen carefully and incorporate their suggestions, changing or adding sticky notes as necessary.

**6** **Draw in dependencies between tasks** A dependency is the relationship between two tasks. The most common type of dependency is end–start (one task ending before the next can start). Dependency can be based either on logic or on resource. Once you have confirmed all tasks are represented and that they are in the right places, take a pen and draw in arrows to represent the dependencies between the tasks required to complete your project.

**7** **Allocate times to tasks** Use the experience of your project team to identify what resources and how much effort will be required to complete each task. Note: this is not how long people need to complete the task ("Calendar time"), but how much effort they will need to put in ("Timesheet time"). Write the time needed for each task into the bottom right-hand field on each sticky note. Where possible, use the same unit of time throughout.

**8** **Assess and resolve risks** Get input from every member of the project team on what they consider to be risks. Give each member of the team two or three sticky notes of a different colour to the ones you have already used, and get them to place them behind the tasks they consider riskiest. Once everyone has placed their notes, facilitate a discussion around their choices, agreeing what countermeasures to adopt and who will be responsible for them.

# Example of a project plan:

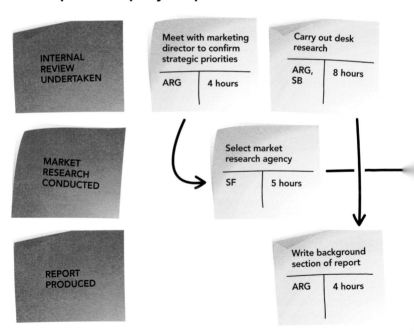

INTERNAL REVIEW UNDERTAKEN

Meet with marketing director to confirm strategic priorities

ARG | 4 hours

Carry out desk research

ARG, SB | 8 hours

MARKET RESEARCH CONDUCTED

Select market research agency

SF | 5 hours

REPORT PRODUCED

Write background section of report

ARG | 4 hours

**9 Allocate tasks** Get your team together and allocate who will do what. People who have been allowed to contribute to the plan in the ways described in steps five to eight will generally have already identified the tasks they would like to work on, or at least recognized that they are the best person to do certain tasks even if they don't want to do them. Simply introduce this step by saying to your team: "Right, who's going to do what?" and then wait for a response. You may be greeted with silence at first, but gradually people will begin to volunteer for tasks. Record names or initials in the bottom left-hand box on each sticky note.

**10 Agree milestones and review points** Take sticky notes of the same colour as those that you used for the products of your project, and place one at the end of each line of tasks. Now facilitate a discussion about when people will be able to complete their tasks and write specific dates (and possibly even times) for when you will review progress. If your project is time-critical, begin with the deadline and work back towards the present; if quality or cost are critical, begin at the present and work forward. Make sure that people cross-check their deadlines with other work or life commitments.

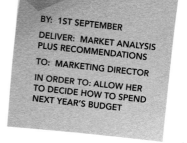

Conduct market research

| Agency | 2 weeks (lapsed time) |
|---|---|

BY: 1ST SEPTEMBER

DELIVER: MARKET ANALYSIS PLUS RECOMMENDATIONS

TO: MARKETING DIRECTOR

IN ORDER TO: ALLOW HER TO DECIDE HOW TO SPEND NEXT YEAR'S BUDGET

Analyze market-research findings and decide on key recommendations

| ARG, SB, SF | 6 hours |
|---|---|

Write final draft report and prepare presentation

| ARG, SB, SF | 6 hours |
|---|---|

Present to marketing director

| ARG, SB | 1 hour |
|---|---|

# Estimating time

Being able to estimate the amount of time required for the tasks and activities of a project is a key skill for any project manager. Indeed, in smaller projects that do not have an explicit budget, keeping to time is likely to be one of the measures of your effectiveness as project manager.

**HOW TO...**
**ESTIMATE THE TIME REQUIRED**

Break down tasks until you know precisely who is doing what.

↓

Involve the person who will be doing the task in deciding how long it will take.

↓

Seek advice from those that have done similar tasks before.

↓

Use a time estimation formula.

## Getting schedules right

In most cases, estimating task times with any degree of accuracy requires a combination of experience and common sense. However, this presupposes that you have correctly identified the task. When projects are late, it is often because activities have not been thought through or recorded properly, so what seemed like a very straightforward task (such as getting a decision from the finance department, for example) gets estimated as a single event rather than a number of small but significant and connected steps, each taking time and effort.

## Involving the team

In most small projects, and certainly in an environment where there are numerous projects running side by side, the challenge is not so much to estimate how much effort tasks will take, but how much time someone needs to be able to complete a task alongside the many other demands made of him/her. Involve team members who will be performing critical tasks in your decision-making process. Ask each person for their estimation of the amount of time they will need to able to complete a certain task, given their other commitments. Be prepared to challenge these estimates if you disagree, but beware of putting undue pressure on people to reduce them.

# Using time estimation formulae

Different organizations, industries, and sectors employ different models or formulae to estimate time. At first sight they always seem mathematical, but in most cases their effectiveness is psychological – either overcoming aversion to estimating, or encouraging more careful thought in those who tend to rush in.

Perhaps the most widely known is the PERT formula (Project Evaluation and Review Technique). To use PERT you need three estimates of the time it could take to complete a task or activity:
- The most likely time required (Tm)
- The most optimistic time assessment (To)
- The most pessimistic time assessment (Tp)

Use the following formula to estimate the most probable duration for that activity (Te):

$$Te = \frac{To + 4Tm + Tp}{6}$$

The formula can be weighted towards pessimism – if the consequences of a late completion of a particular task are severe, for example – by reducing the Tm multiplier and adding a Tp multiplier:

$$Te = \frac{To + 3Tm + 2Tp}{6}$$

# Representing the plan

Once created, your project plan should become your main point of reference for managing progress during the control phase of the project. It is a living document, and you should expect that it will be updated through several versions to keep up with changing circumstances and to take account of incorrect estimates of time or cost.

## Making a digital record

For most projects, you will want to represent your project using a software package rather than on paper. This gives your plan a more professional look and makes it easier to store and to communicate to others; and it allows you to automatically calculate items such as overall cost, critical path duration, and resource requirements. Using software, a single plan can easily be converted into a number of formats so that different aspects of the project are highlighted. In addition, the impact of changes or variances can more easily be tested, and multiple versions can be held for comparison.

There are many types of software package available, each with their own strengths and weaknesses. Choosing the right one for your needs will depend on the size and complexity of your project, the experience of the project team, and the software to which they all have access. As a general rule, ensure that managing the software you choose will not get in the way of managing the project itself, and that everyone will have first-hand access to the sections of the plan relevant to their work.

**? ASK YOURSELF...**
**WHAT ARE MY REQUIREMENTS?**

- What aspects of the plan will I need to analyze and when?
- In what circumstances will I need to present or discuss the plan?
- How often will it need updating?
- Who else needs to have access to the plan?
- What representation will be most easily accessible and understood by them?

## CHOOSING SOFTWARE

| SOFTWARE PACKAGE TYPE | STRENGTHS | WEAKNESSES |
|---|---|---|
| **Specialist project management software** Ideal for a specialist project environment where people are familiar with its use and can read all formats and representations intuitively. | • Allows you to make multiple representations of the plan<br>• Calendar facility allows longer-term scheduling<br>• Shows dependencies between tasks<br>• Integrates schedule, budget, and resource plans<br>• Allows automatic calculation of critical path and resource implications | • "Occasional" project managers may spend more time learning to use the software than actually using it<br>• Over-sophisticated for small projects<br>• Does not readily integrate project work and day-to-day activities |
| **Spreadsheet software** Useful for simpler projects and where managing a budget is important. | • Widely available, so most stakeholders will be able to access the plan<br>• Flexible for smaller projects<br>• Allows automatic calculation of durations and costs using formulae<br>• Graphical representation of tasks is possible | • Requires specialist knowledge to represent more complex information<br>• Does not readily integrate project work and day-to-day activities |
| **Graphics packages** Useful for communicating the plan to project stakeholders as a presentation, and for highlighting the relationships between tasks. | • Good for making a professional-looking representation of your plan<br>• Has multiple options for representing products, tasks, and responsibilities<br>• Project templates available in many packages | • Not universally available, so some stakeholders may not be able to access the plan<br>• Has no automatic interface with diary or financial packages, so schedules/budgets require manual updating when adjustments are made |
| **Diary and tasklist software** Ideal for a multi-project environment or where people have to integrate project work with day-to-day business as usual; and for small projects with no cash budget. | • Easy integration between project and day-to-day work<br>• Good at representing the schedule<br>• Widely available<br>• A familiar format for most project stakeholders | • Not good at representing critical path, resource plans, or budgets<br>• No automatic tie-in with budgeting software<br>• Does not allow you to show the relationships between tasks graphically |

# Chapter 3

# **Managing work in progress**

Management during the control phase, once a project is under way, requires a sophisticated skill-set that includes team leadership, delegation and communication, budget and schedule management, and high performance under pressure.

# Making time for the project

Project management is rarely a full-time role, except in large or specialist organizations. Finding time for your longer-term work is often one of the biggest challenges faced by managers of smaller projects, especially when the planning stage ends and hands-on work begins.

## **Recognizing your priorities**

Most modern approaches to time management address our tendency to prioritize urgency over importance when deciding what to do on a day-to-day basis. While the ability to react to unforeseen problems is essential, being purely "reactive" damages productivity, reduces the quality of results, and not least is stressful for you.

As a project manager your focus has to be further ahead than the immediate; hence the emphasis on definition and planning, on proactive communication with all stakeholders, and on risk analysis.

**TIP**

**GET ORGANIZED**

Plan regular two-hour slots of project time in your diary. Set yourself a specific task to do in that time one week ahead, and then prepare as you would for an exam, gathering the information and resources you need to complete the task successfully.

# Finding your focus

Finding time to focus on the big picture is the key to integrating your long-term role and responsibilities with the short-term demands of your project.

• Start with a plan: begin every day by spending five to ten minutes getting a handle on your agenda for that day. Identify time already allocated to meetings and other fixed tasks. Allocate time to the tasks you plan to do off your "to do" list. Plan in enough flexibility to deal with the unexpected, and at least one review point at which you can check your direction and make adjustments.

• Integrate project tasks with your day-to-day tasks and diary. Do this by recording them on the same list and ensuring they are broken down to around the same size. If the average task size on your "to do" list is 15–30 minutes, for example, don't have project tasks of four hours in length – they won't get done.

• Motivate yourself to do longer-term tasks every day. Set yourself a goal of doing one longer-term task per day on each of your projects, or one task preparing for the next deliverable (i.e. not the current one) on every project.

## ✔ CHECKLIST **MANAGING YOUR TIME**

|  | YES | NO |
|---|---|---|
| • Do you allocate "interruption-free" time in your diary, when you get away from your desk and turn off your email and phone, for tasks that require uninterrupted thought? | ☐ | ☐ |
| • Do you factor reactive time – spent responding to emails and phonecalls and attending ad-hoc meetings – into your day-to-day planning? | ☐ | ☐ |
| • Do you discourage reactive requests? | ☐ | ☐ |
| • Do you delegate work early and effectively? | ☐ | ☐ |
| • Do you ensure, where possible, that meetings begin on time and stick to the agenda? | ☐ | ☐ |

# Delegating effectively

Set time aside on a regular basis to plan which tasks and activities can be delegated to others. This may not be restricted to project tasks: in order to have the time for project management, you may find that you have to delegate other parts of your job, too.

## Getting delegation right

Successful delegation is not always easy, especially if you are managing a small project within a multi-project environment. As the manager of a small project you can expect to find yourself delegating longer-term tasks to busy people who may only have partial understanding of what you are trying to achieve, and for whom your project is a relatively low priority. When deciding which tasks and activities to delegate, take time to consider the benefits you could expect from delegating a particular task, and the blocks that you would need to overcome. Once you have identified potential opportunities for delegation, clarify the specifics of how you could achieve them by asking yourself:

• What is the required outcome or deliverable from delegating this task?
• Why is this important?
• How will it be used and when is it required by?
• What constraints are there on how the result can be achieved?
• What could go wrong?
• Who should I delegate this task to?
• Why should they do it?
• What objections might I need to overcome?
• What help will they need?
• What level of authority can they handle?

**BEAT INDECISION**
Try to make quick decisions as to who to approach and what precisely has to be done, and don't procrastinate about approaching the sponsor if their involvement is required.

**FIGHT GUILT**
Nice people don't like delegating unpleasant tasks. However, effective leadership requires a hard head as well as a soft heart.

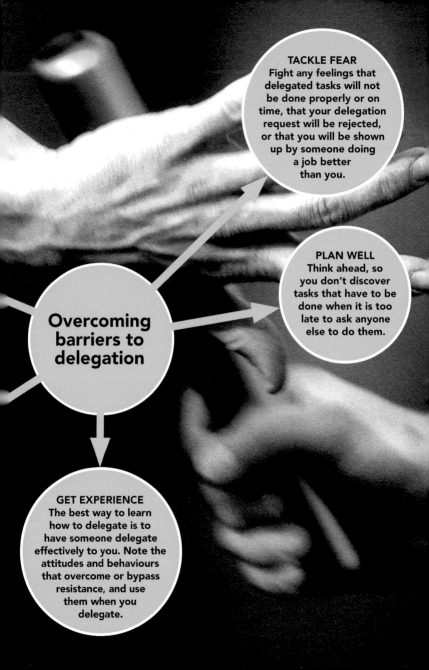

**Overcoming barriers to delegation**

**TACKLE FEAR**
Fight any feelings that delegated tasks will not be done properly or on time, that your delegation request will be rejected, or that you will be shown up by someone doing a job better than you.

**PLAN WELL**
Think ahead, so you don't discover tasks that have to be done when it is too late to ask anyone else to do them.

**GET EXPERIENCE**
The best way to learn how to delegate is to have someone delegate effectively to you. Note the attitudes and behaviours that overcome or bypass resistance, and use them when you delegate.

# Preparing to delegate

Where possible, delegate straight from the plan: as soon as you have identified a task that needs to be done, select someone to do it. If they are present when the task is identified, use that moment to pass responsibility to them. Give delegatees as much warning as possible: it is preferable to have three weeks' warning of a deadline, rather than three days. Warn people of impending delegation, even before you are clear on what you want done. Brevity is of the essence and it's not a bad idea to use a standard format for this "heads-up message" (see right).

# Setting the details

Arrange a formal meeting with the person you are delegating the task to. The success of the task depends on your ability to transmit the details and parameters of the task to the delegatee at this meeting. When delegating complex tasks, in particular, it is vital that you are confident that your colleague has fully understood and is committed to what they have been asked to do. Asking "Do you understand?" is simply not good enough: it is a closed question and as such will generally receive just a "yes" or "no" answer. Instead, try to ask

## HOW TO...
## COMPOSE A HEADS-UP MESSAGE

DEFINE THE SCOPE OF THE TASK
Give a general description of the task to be delegated, e.g. "I've got some figures I need you to analyze."

↓

SET A TIMEFRAME
Describe when work is likely to start and when it will be needed, e.g. "I will brief you on Monday for a deadline on Friday. The task should take about four hours."

↓

ASK THE DELEGATEE TO PREPARE
Let the person know what they can be doing to prepare themselves for the work, e.g. "Can you set aside that amount of time next week?"

↓

SET A MEETING DATE
Give a time and a place for a delegation meeting, e.g. "We'll meet in the boardroom on Monday at 10am. Please bring your diary."

open questions, such as "How do you plan to do this?" This will give you more information about their level of understanding, but it can be quite challenging for the delegatee to answer without time to reflect. The following model for holding a split delegation meeting has proven successful in delegating project tasks to some very difficult characters.

# Holding a split meeting

Organize your delegation meeting in two parts separated by a "gap" to give the delegatee time to reflect before being invited to explain how they will approach their task.

• **Part one** Describe what is required, by when, and at what cost; why it is required; and the context and parameters of what is required, including any restrictions on the methods to be adopted. By giving people whole jobs or the context of the whole job you will increase people's understanding and motivation leading to a more satisfactory outcome all round.

• **Gap** Give your colleague time for reflection on their own. Create the gap with a statement such as: "Let me get us a cup of coffee while you stay here and have a think about the task. When I come back you can tell me how you're going to go about doing it and what help you'll need from me."

• **Part two** Ask your colleague to brief you on any modifications they feel should be made to the goal (where appropriate); the way they plan to approach the task; what help they will need from you; and when they would like to review progress.

Once delegation is compete, give your colleague immediate feedback on their contribution, and pass a summary on to their manager where appropriate.

**TIP**

**DON'T SKIP THE GAP**

Creating thinking time within a formal meeting structure is important. Although people sometimes protest that they want "time to digest" or that they "haven't got time right now", giving them immediate time for reflection is always worthwhile.

## IN FOCUS... GIVING FEEDBACK

Longer-term delegation benefits greatly from formal (diarized) review and follow-up sessions. Follow the adage: "People don't do what you expect – they do what you inspect!" Ad-hoc checking is generally sloppy and inefficient – in fact, imprecise questions such as: "How are things going?" result in inexact answers, such as: "Oh, fine!", and almost invariably lead to problems at completion with missed deadlines or partial delivery. When reviewing a delegatee's work, accept what is good enough, don't criticize irrelevant details. Accept that a task may have been done differently to how you would have done it.

# Maintaining momentum

Project work often requires effort over a prolonged period with little to show for it, so maintaining motivation can be a challenge. Procrastination is an ever-present danger, particularly on tasks that require high levels of concentration or challenging conversations with colleagues or clients.

**DON'T PROCRASTINATE**

Avoid putting off challenging tasks – every time you do so, you put a brake on your motivation for the project as a whole.

## Motivating yourself

Before you can start to motivate your team, you first have to motivate yourself; if you are not enthusiastic there is little chance that others will be. Do this by a combination of revisiting the end result – reminding yourself of its value and what it will be like to achieve it – and monitoring progress. Be alive to the first signs of procrastination and act quickly to ensure internal resistance is never given the chance to build up.

# Beating mental blocks

Sometimes you can reach a point of near paralysis on a task. If this happens, try using this technique for re-energizing yourself: take a blank piece of paper and write the task on it. Then write for three minutes continuously about the task. Keep the pen moving, and jot down anything that comes to mind: why the task needs to be done; why you haven't done it; who else is involved; other ways of doing it; and steps to dealing with it. Now go through what you have written and highlight any insights or action points. Decide what one thing you will do immediately to progress the task – and then do it. Most people report an immediate rise in energy which, coupled with an increased understanding of the task, enables them to get over what had built into an insurmountable hurdle in their mind.

# Motivating others

Motivating members of your project team can be difficult for a number of reasons:
• Long-term deadlines are always in danger of being pushed into the background by the distractions and crises of the day-to-day workload.
• Non-routine tasks are prone to procrastination.

## HOW TO... MOTIVATE YOUR TEAM

Break the project down into meaningful products that can be completed on a regular enough basis to maintain a sense of progress.

↓

Be open about the possibility of procrastination and discuss ways to overcome it.

↓

Always delegate in the context of the overall project.

↓

Find an engaging way to represent progress, rather than just marking ticks on a list (stars on a chart, perhaps, or sweets from a jar).

• Team members may not see a connection between their effort on tasks, the project achieving its objective, and any benefit to them.
• People with a hierarchical mindset may resent doing work for a project manager who is less senior than them. Approach such people positively, but be prepared to escalate a problem as soon as you recognize that it will be beyond your capability to deal with it.

Take positive steps to motivate your team (see above), but also use your risk assessment to identify points where momentum may be lost, recording potential counter-measures in the risk log.

# Communicating successfully

As the project manager, you are the hub of all communication within the project team and between the project team and the outside world. At different stages of the project you will find yourself dealing with different stakeholders, but the three constant axes of communication you need to maintain are with the sponsor, the client, and the team.

**TIP**

**PASS ON KEY INFORMATION**
Operate a "no surprises" policy in your dealings with the sponsor – he or she should never have to say "You should have told me about this before."

## Engaging your sponsor and client

Communication with the sponsor should be characterized by a high level of openness and trust from the start of the project. Spend time establishing how your communication will work. Discuss scheduled communication (such as diarized review meetings) and agree on when and how you expect ad-hoc communication to take place. Give warning of any decisions that need to be made and present facts to the sponsor in a written form for consideration. Record notes of all meetings, in particular any action points.

Communication with the client will tend to be more formal than with the sponsor. The challenge is often to be assertive, particularly when requesting decisions, access, or information. As with the sponsor, give the client notice of any decisions. The client relationship can occasionally contain an element of politics, particularly if the client is under pressure from members of his or her organization. As a general rule, aim to do everything you can to make your client look good. If it becomes apparent that this is not possible, use the sponsor to bypass the obstacle.

**? ASK YOURSELF...**
**AM I A GOOD LISTENER?**

- Do I quieten my self-talk, so that I can focus on the speaker and understand his or her perspective?
- Do I clarify vague statements, to find out whether what the person is saying is factually and logically correct?
- Do I try to assess how people are feeling, and ask probing questions to understand what lies behind those emotions?

# Talking to your team

Maintain an open and honest relationship with your team. In large teams, there is always a danger of some people being left out of the loop when decisions are made or new information becomes available. Make sure you have accurate distribution lists set up for email and documents. On larger and longer-running projects, you may find it helpful to post general information on an intranet site to which team members have access.

# Choosing the method

Care is needed when selecting the medium by which you will communicate a particular message. Sending a sensitive message by email, for example, runs the risk of a potentially damaging misunderstanding with the recipient. Before pressing "send", take time to think about your purpose in communicating, what you want the outcome to be, and how "complex" the message is in emotional and intellectual terms.

## Selecting a medium for your message

**HIGH**

**Emotional complexity**

**Message:** simple but emotionally charged, possibly requiring action from the recipient

**Medium:**
• Ad-hoc meeting
• Telephone conversation

**Message:** complex, with a high risk of misunderstanding or hurt feelings; need for the recipient to buy in to an idea and perhaps take action

**Medium:**
• Formal meeting
• Video conference

**Message:** simple, with a low risk of misunderstanding or hurt feelings; no need for high levels of emotional buy in

**Medium:**
• Voicemail message
• Email
• Note on the desk

**Message:** intellectually complex but emotionally non-contentious facts and figures

**Medium:**
• Fax
• Email
• Letter
• Memorandum

**LOW**       Intellectual complexity       **HIGH**

# Reviewing progress

Getting the team together is costly in both time and resources, but well-run review meetings are an essential ingredient in any project, offering you the opportunity to check past progress and confirm future direction. They also renew people's identification with your project team.

## Keeping track of progress

An effective review meeting should be one part of a continuous cycle of activity. Prior to every meeting, each team member should work towards completing their tasks, and if they fail to do this within the set timeframe, non-completion should be reported to you. Use this information to formulate and circulate an agenda for the review meeting, with minutes of the last meeting attached as preparatory reading. At the meeting, start by discussing progress since your last

## RUNNING SUCCESSFUL REVIEWS

**FAST TRACK** | **OFF TRACK**
--- | ---
Sending the agenda for the meeting in advance | Holding ad-hoc review meetings with no preparation
Ensuring that agenda items run to time, without having to be rushed | Allowing the discussion to wander and side issues to dominate
Allocating action points to attendees with agreed deadlines | Assuming that everyone will know what they have to do
Finishing with a discussion about what has been learnt for next time | Accepting excuses without discussing how things can change

✔ # CHECKLIST **PREPARING TO CHAIR A REVIEW MEETING**

| | YES | NO |
|---|---|---|
| • Are you up to date with all aspects of your own project work? (If your project work is behind schedule, you won't have the authority to chase others for theirs.) | ☐ | ☐ |
| • Do you know who will be there and how they are doing with the tasks they have been set? | ☐ | ☐ |
| • Have you set aside extra time so that you can arrange the room and set up equipment before other people arrive? | ☐ | ☐ |
| • Are you feeling calm? (If you are stressed, this is likely to rub off on other people.) | ☐ | ☐ |
| • Are you prepared to challenge people who have not done what they are committed to, or who are behaving in a disruptive manner? | ☐ | ☐ |

review, then make decisions about what tasks need to be completed before the next time you meet. Delegate specific actions to individuals. Record these actions in "Action minutes", which should be circulated as soon after the meeting as possible to give people the best chance of completing their tasks prior to the next meeting.

## Scheduling review meetings

Review meetings can be scheduled as a regular event – at the same time of every day, for example, or on the same day of every week or month. Alternatively, the meetings can be fixed to the expected delivery date of certain products or to stages of the project. Both of these approaches have their strengths and weaknesses: regular meetings in the same place and at the same time are more prone to "game playing" and a lack of concentration amongst attendees, but meetings set by the delivery dates of your project are more difficult to schedule to ensure that everyone can attend.

**TIP**

**KEEP IT BRIEF**
During busy periods, hold short "stand-up" review meetings early in the day, or at a point when most people would expect to be taking a break. Insist on a prompt start, brief contributions, and no deviation from the main purpose of reviewing progress and coordinating activity through the next period.

# Managing project information

"Filing" lacks the star quality of other aspects of project work and rarely rates in people's top three most enjoyable or rewarding job roles. Nevertheless, if you want to be in full control of your project, management of paper-based and electronic information is essential.

## Assembling your project file

Set up a project folder or filing system to manage your project documentation as part of the initiation phase of your project. Compile a checklist – the document schedule – listing the records that it contains, and place this at the front of your project file. This will enable anyone looking for a document to see at a glance whether it is in the file. Use the

### The contents of a project file

### 1 DOCUMENT SCHEDULE

Like the index in a book, the document schedule should tell you at a glance what paperwork the file contains. It can be a useful checklist: score through the documents that are not needed and put the date of entry for any document you put into the file

### 4 CHANGES TO SCOPE RECORDS

Keep these records close to the definition documents so that the material they contain is always accessed alongside the original scope to which they refer.

### 5 PROJECT PLAN AND BUDGET

Always keep the baseline plan and budget in the file, along with the most up-to-date versions. Archive intermediate versions elsewhere to avoid confusion.

**TIP**

**TAG YOUR DOCUMENTS**

Use different colours of paper for different types of document (minutes, sign-offs, etc.), and mark every project document with the date/time of creation and a version number from the outset.

document schedule to structure your conversation with the sponsor about the various records that will be required at different points in the project.

Even small projects can generate large amounts of paperwork, so it is important that you plan how you will organize the contents of your file. Version control can be helpful, because the drafting and signing-off processes can generate multiple versions of individual documents. Mark every document with a version number, and keep archive versions (back copies you are keeping pending a final review, for example) in a separate part of the project file from "reference" information – such as the current project plan – that is in regular use.

File active documents (those requiring a specific future action) in date order using a "Bring Forward" file, and use the reminder system in your electronic task list or calendar to flag important dates.

## 2 TEAM ORGANIZATION CHART

Keep a chart setting out who is doing what in your team. This allows anyone examining the file to see who they should approach on a particular matter. Include contact information and distribution lists.

## 3 DEFINITION DOCUMENTS

Keep a suite of documents that set out the definition of your project. This may include the mandate, brief, business case, PID, and any legal contracts or client agreements.

## 6 RISK LOG

You will refer to this document almost as often as you do to your plan and budget, so make sure you keep the risk log in your project file up to date with constant review.

## 7 THE MINUTES OF REVIEW MEETINGS

Keep records of minutes that include live action points or significant points of reference in the project file. Archive all others to ensure the file doesn't become cluttered or confused.

# Monitoring costs

While it is important for you to monitor the schedule of the project and maintain focus on the outcome, it is equally vital that you keep track of the costs your project is incurring. Failure to do so can result in a project that, while seemingly successful is, in fact, uneconomic.

**TIP**

**DON'T IGNORE HIDDEN COSTS**

Beware the seductive but potentially false logic: "We don't have the budget for that, we'll do it ourselves."

## Managing project accounts

Effective cost monitoring throughout the lifecycle of a project is important for a number of reasons: it enables you to give the sponsor a true picture of progress whenever you are asked for it; it reduces risk by ensuring decisions to modify or cancel the project are taken early; it identifies areas of inefficiency; and it provides valuable information for planning future projects. Keeping track of your costs is also important because it could highlight theft or fraud. Like any other pot of money, project budgets occasionally attract criminal attention. If you are the person responsible for controlling expenditure, you may be liable unless you can demonstrate that you have used suitable procedures for monitoring costs.

## CASE STUDY

### Adjusting to change

The property department in a law firm won a contract to review 6,000 files for a local government agency. They priced the job at £900k, based on two hours per file after a start-up period. This proved accurate – experienced team members took just under two hours per file. However, the volume of work and tight schedule meant that morale dipped and staff turnover increased. The constant need to induct new staff pushed the average time per file for the first thousand files up to 2 hours 15 minutes. This would have caused the contract to overshoot by 12.5 per cent, costing the firm £112.5k in lost revenue. The head of the department negotiated secondments from other departments to spread the workload, and offered incentives to raise morale. Thanks to the early intervention, productivity returned to less than two hours per file, and the project hit its projected profit margin.

# Keeping track of costs

If you are managing a small project, you may not have a budget for out-of-pocket costs – paid to external organizations for materials or services – but you would do well to keep track of the invisible cost of the work undertaken by your internal team. Particularly in a multi-project environment, timesheets provide a mechanism for charging costs back to the right client or cost centre.

Out-of-pocket costs generally attract heavy scrutiny. Nevertheless this budget can come under pressure either because of inaccurate estimates at the definition stage, additional features added to the scope without parallel increases in the budget, or poor risk management. If you are responsible for the budget, ensure you are clear on the reasons for any unforeseen expenditure before authorizing payment. Check the impact on other aspects of the budget: are you using money for desirable but non-essential features, leaving later essential features under-funded?

# Dealing with cost overruns

Not every cost overrun is serious – sometimes costs run ahead of plan simply because work is progressing more quickly than anticipated. On other occasions, you may have underestimated the cost of a "one-off" item of expenditure, but feel this is likely to be offset by an overestimate elsewhere. The point at which even a minor overspend should be taken seriously is when it is early warning that you have underestimated a whole class of activity upon which the project depends. Tell the sponsor as soon as you perceive that unforeseen costs may require an increase in the overall project budget. If the budget is fixed (critical), identify any non-essential features you can remove from the scope to bring costs back in line.

## HOW TO... MONITOR INVISIBLE COSTS

Use a timesheet system to keep track of time spent by your internal team.

Allocate a financial value to the time recorded on the timesheets.

Base calculations on the worker's salary broken down into an hourly rate.

Add in the overhead cost of employing that person (heating, lighting, office space, etc.)

# Managing changes to scope

It is sometimes necessary to change or re-scope a project in order to adapt to circumstances that were not known when you drew up the definition. You must manage these changes carefully to avoid any misunderstanding between you, your sponsor, and the client.

## Defining the change

The golden rule when re-scoping a project is to agree all changes of scope in writing with the project sponsor. By creating a written record of all changes you create an audit trail that ensures that you and the sponsor have the same understanding of what the change is and why you are making it. Never agree to a change in scope before carrying out a full impact assessment, to identify how other features of the product will be affected, and developing a costed plan for how to deliver the change.

Communicate changes to all those involved in the project's delivery as well as those who will receive the end product. If your organization does not have a standard "Changes to Scope" document format and you decide to create one, ensure it has a similar format to the original scoping document so that the two can be compared easily and the specific modifications highlighted. The document should be signed off by the client – to ensure that he or she wants the change; by you, to confirm that you can deliver it; and by the sponsor who ultimately has the authority to sanction the change.

### IN FOCUS...
#### SCOPE CREEP

The term "scope creep" is a term used to describe uncontrolled changes to the scope of a project. It is described as "creep" because the changes happen in such small steps that they go unnoticed until their true impact becomes apparent in the run-up to implementation. Sloppy project managers sometimes blame "scope creep" when they fail to deliver features that they should have spotted in the initial brief. However, it can also be caused by clients changing their minds or trying to get more than they have paid for in a commercial project.

# Common reasons for changes to a project's scope

**USAGE CHANGE**
The circumstances in which the end product will be used have changed.

**INDECISION**
The client changes their mind about what they want.

**NEW PERSONNEL**
The client changes (a new person comes in with new ideas).

**LOSS OF RESOURCES**
The resources available to the project change (the budget is cut or increased, for example, or people with vital skills are moved out of or into the project team).

**A RISK GOES BAD**
The technology doesn't work, for example, or a legal hurdle cannot be overcome.

**POOR PLANNING**
It becomes apparent that the original scope is impossible to deliver within the set time or cost constraints.

**ADDED BENEFITS**
New facts or technological advances would enable the project to deliver valuable additional benefits if the scope were modified.

# Chapter 4
# **Going live**

At the end of every project, there comes a point at which whatever it has produced needs to be handed over to the end users. As the culmination of all your efforts, this should be an exciting time for the project manager, but there will also be challenges to face, and careful management is required to deliver a smooth handover and a successful outcome.

# Implementing the project

Ensuring that the client, the team, and your organization have a positive experience as your project "goes live" is one of a project manager's most important responsibilities. The decisions you make during every phase of your project's lifecycle should be with implementation in mind.

## **Overcoming challenges**

Implementation is primarily a client-focused phase of a project. However, you should also consider its significance for the end user, the project team, and your organization. As the project goes live, end users have to assimilate changes and come out of their comfort zone, while project team members have to let go of a project and move on to something new. Your organization simply wants swift and trouble-free implementation in order to realize the benefits of their investment. Your role as project manager is to help all three groups deal with these challenges.

# KEY ACTIONS FOR SUCCESSFUL IMPLEMENTATION

| PHASE OF PROJECT | ACTIONS |
|---|---|
| **Initiation phase** Describe the issue to be addressed or opportunity to be exploited. | • Conduct research among end users to establish how widespread the issue or opportunity is. <br> • Document findings and, where confidentiality allows, circulate them to those who contributed. |
| **Definition phase** Design an end product that satisfies the need identified in initiation. | • Wherever possible, design the product in consultation with the client/end user – attribute good ideas to those who offered them. <br> • Give an indicative date for implementation. <br> • Use prototypes and mock-ups to bring the idea alive both for the client and the project team. |
| **Planning phase** Design a communications plan that delivers the information that different stakeholders need; and ensure the resources are available for successful implementation. | • Find out what aspects of progress the stakeholders are interested in and how frequently they want reports, then create a communications plan to deliver this. <br> • Plan in time and budget for implementation activities such as rehearsals, marketing, training, and change management. <br> • Book facilities, equipment, and personnel required for implementation as soon as you have a launch timetable. |
| **Control phase** Ensure all stakeholders are kept informed on progress and manage people's expectations. | • Deliver the communications plan, and take advantage of any unexpected opportunities to promote your project. <br> • Find opportunities for listening to stakeholders' hopes and concerns. <br> • Tell all stakeholders about any changes to the product or launch date, explaining why these have occurred. <br> • Create the materials (documentation, guides, manuals, etc.) required to support implementation. <br> • Train those who will support the product once it has gone live. <br> • Recruit end users who will test the product as soon as it is ready for implementation. <br> • Plan and rehearse implementation events. |
| **Implementation phase** Present the product in the most positive way possible, demonstrating an understanding of all stakeholders' needs. | • Get end users to test what you have produced (User Acceptance Testing). <br> • Hold implementation events to roll out the end product. <br> • Train or brief end users and distribute supporting documentation as necessary. <br> • Get the sponsor to inspect the finished product and sign it off as complete. <br> • Hold a celebratory event with the project team. <br> • Reassign project personnel, providing feedback to them and their managers as appropriate. |

# Preparing for handover

Although the majority of work has been done, projects can sometimes stall at the implementation stage. You may run out of budget, or lose members of your team to other projects, or there may be last-minute changes from the client as they realize that implementation is imminent. Careful management at this stage ensures that your handover to the end users goes as smoothly as possible.

## Managing the final stages

**HOLD ON TO YOUR TEAM**
Tell team members that they are finished on your project only when you are absolutely clear that this is the case.

As a project nears completion, team members can often feel jaded; the novelty that drew them to the project in the first place has become a distant memory. To reinvigorate your team, hold a pre-implementation meeting with all those involved, including clients and end users wherever possible. The core purpose of this meeting is to produce a detailed route map through to completion, but a well-run meeting can do wonders for your team's motivation and focus – especially if they see the client's enthusiasm for what you are about to deliver.

## HOW TO...
## HOLD A PRE-IMPLEMENTATION MEETING

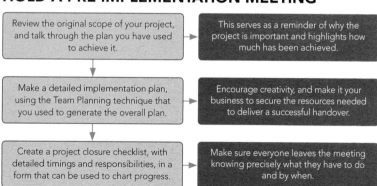

Review the original scope of your project, and talk through the plan you have used to achieve it.

This serves as a reminder of why the project is important and highlights how much has been achieved.

Make a detailed implementation plan, using the Team Planning technique that you used to generate the overall plan.

Encourage creativity, and make it your business to secure the resources needed to deliver a successful handover.

Create a project closure checklist, with detailed timings and responsibilities, in a form that can be used to chart progress.

Make sure everyone leaves the meeting knowing precisely what they have to do and by when.

# Steering the end game

Your role in the lead up to implementation is primarily one of problem solving and coordination of the activity required for the project to "go live". Get round and see all stakeholders, particularly team members. Show an interest in what they are doing but resist the temptation to step in unless they really cannot do what has been asked of them without your help. Increase the frequency of review as you get close to your final date, but do not allow these meetings to get in the way of the work they should be doing. If everyone is in the same building, for example, a 10-minute "stand-up" meeting may work best, while conference calls are a sensible alternative for multi-site projects.

# Running final tests

For some projects, User Acceptance Testing* is one of the last steps before implementation. Most frequently found in software development, UAT can be applied in a variety of situations. The testing is carried out by a representative panel of end users, who work through as many different scenarios as necessary to be sure that the product will perform as expected when it goes live. UAT must not be used to confirm that the product is what the end users want – that should have been defined in the project scope and any subsequent "changes to scope" documents.

*User Acceptance Testing (UAT) — the final technical test of a product, to make sure that it works as it is supposed to.

# Handing the project over

The way in which a project "goes live" varies from project to project depending on the nature of its product. With time-critical projects there is rarely any doubt about the "go live" point, but where quality is the critical factor the opposite is often the case, and it takes a conscious effort to mark the point at which a project is complete.

**TIP**

**TAKE ADVICE**

Speak to your sponsor about your plans for marking "go live". Ultimately it is up to him or her to decide when the project is complete.

## Signalling the end point

Projects are different to business as usual because they have an end point at which they can be declared complete and then have their success evaluated. Even if you are the only person working on a project, it is still helpful to mark the "go live" point, to signal that the project is finished before moving on.

For most projects, implementation should coincide with the transference of responsibility from the project team to an ongoing support function. Perversely, the better you and your team have been at managing the client while the project was underway, the more difficult you will find it to get them to transfer their allegiance to a new group. By marking the "go live" point, you make a definitive statement to your client that the time has come for this to happen.

## ✔ CHECKLIST **MARKING "GO LIVE"**

|  | YES | NO |
|---|---|---|
| • Have I made a clear declaration to all stakeholders that the project is complete? | ☐ | ☐ |
| • Have I clearly signalled to the client and end users that they are now responsible for the product? | ☐ | ☐ |
| • Have I marked the point at which project personnel are available for other assignments? | ☐ | ☐ |
| • Have I taken the opportunity to say thank you to those who have contributed to the project? | ☐ | ☐ |

**CASE STUDY**

**Oiling the wheels**

A project manager charged with moving 40 people from an office in the heart of the West End of London to more spacious but cheaper premises in a less affluent part of London faced a challenge to ensure smooth implementation: the move was for financial reasons and no-one wanted to go. He decided to put together a welcome pack for each member of staff, and asked every shop, bar, café, restaurant, and gym in the area around the new offices whether they would make introductory offers to the newcomers on production of their company ID cards. On the day of the move, he placed the finished pack – worth approximately £100 of discounted goods and services – on each desk in the new offices. The offers it contained actively encouraged people to explore the area rather than simply sitting at their desks and complaining about their new surroundings. And when they did take up the offers, they found that they were welcomed as valuable additional custom.

# Holding an event

Hold a "go live" event (perhaps couched as a final review meeting) in which you review the whole project. Evaluate the changes and benefits it has achieved. Consider how you can organize or stage manage the event so that there are things for people to see, do, and talk about. However, the watchword is appropriateness – if you over-play "go live" you lay yourself open to accusations of self-promotion. Involve the project sponsor in the event – get him or her to offer an assessment of the project and thank all those who have contributed.

Another pretext for an event might be to introduce the client or end users to the people who are about to take on responsibility for supporting them. Reiterate the post-implementation support that will be available and how snagging will take place. Snagging is the process of identifying and resolving minor defects that takes place during the implementation phase, prior to the project being declared complete. Make sure that everyone understands the part you need them to play in bedding the project in.

# Providing support

In a quality-critical project, the quality of post-implementation support given to the end user is essential to its long-term success. Never declare a project complete until the end user has been trained to use the product and first-line support is available from outside the project team.

# Evaluating success

Once the end product has been delivered, the project manager's final act should be to review the outcome of the project and evaluate its overall success. It can often be illuminating to make this post-implementation review against both the original scope and any subsequent modifications.

## Analyzing the outcome

You should review the success of your project in a number of ways. Firstly, look at your immediate impression: did the project deliver what was expected? This level of review is best done at the same time as implementation – indeed it should be part of the sign-off procedure involving sponsor, client, and project manager. The review process should also look at whether the project has delivered a long-term benefit. In time-critical projects, this may already be at least partly evident at implementation or shortly afterwards, but in quality-critical projects the benefits may take longer to become clear. Finally, your evaluation should look at the benefits gained in business terms. Was the project worth it financially?

**TIP**

**INVOLVE THE SPONSOR**

Try to get the sponsor involved in the review process – experience suggests that without their involvement, the review rarely gets done as people are busy and move on to the next job.

**EXPRESS YOUR THANKS**

Hand write a personal letter to each team member expressing thanks for his or her personal contribution, making the effort to write something different in each one.

**COMMEMORATE THE OCCASION**

Have a team photograph taken or a group caricature drawn, create a collage of memorable moments, or frame an appropriate piece of the project plan and give it to each team member with a hand-written comment.

# Ideas for celebrating success

## GIVE A PROJECT GIFT
Give an inscribed desk ornament, to thank people for taking part. This does not have to be expensive but should be tasteful, fun, and/or useful. A distinctive pen or mug often stays around for a long time if the associations with the project were positive ones.

## GIVE BONUSES
Team members will always appreciate a cash bonus, if funds are available.

## GIVE A PERSONAL REWARD
Send an appropriate gift to members of the team at their homes with a personalized note: a bottle of Champagne, a bunch of flowers, vouchers for a spa, or tickets for an event can all deliver a far bigger message than the money that they cost.

## ALLOCATE FUNDS
Put a small "celebration fund" into the project budget, which increases or decreases depending on whether the project is in front or behind time and budget. At the end of the project, hold a social event, involving everyone who contributed, at which you and the sponsor (and client if appropriate) can express your thanks.

# Reviewing the process

A "lessons learnt" review allows you to learn from the process you have been through and helps you find ways to improve your project management. Because the project process should be repeatable, the main purpose of review is to establish what went well, what could have gone better, and what you can do to improve future projects.

## Looking back at your project

The review process is your chance to learn from experience. It is not just about spotting errors or identifying parts of the process that did not run as smoothly as they could have – evaluation of what was successful is equally informative. If something worked particularly well (such as a technique or a supplier), it should be noted for future reference.

However, inevitably there will be some things that go wrong in your projects, and these also provide valuable lessons for the future. Although they may have been unforeseeable the first time they occurred, by taking the time to understand what has happened and why, you should be able to gain insights that would otherwise be missed, and take action to prevent their recurrence in future projects.

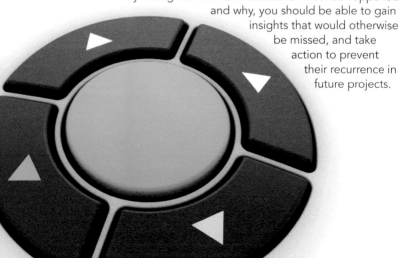

# PLANNING PROJECTS FOR LEARNING

| FAST TRACK | OFF TRACK |
|---|---|
| Establishing quality assurance procedures from the outset | Allowing an experienced project team to perform their roles out of habit |
| Giving personal learning objectives for the project to all team members | Being cynical about the organization's ability to do things differently |
| Including "lessons learnt" as a regular agenda item for meetings | Considering change a threat to what has been successful in the past |
| Having a team culture characterized by high levels of feedback | Allowing a blame culture, in which it is dangerous to admit mistakes |
| Establishing mechanisms for disseminating new ideas | Holding the project plan centrally and discouraging discussion of its details |

# Learning from the details

When reviewing the project, consider all aspects of the process in detail. Do not rely on opinions about what went well or make assumptions about what went wrong: talk to those involved and try to discover the facts. When these are in dispute, ask for evidence. Be curious about why things happened, and explore how this could inform future project decisions. When searching for the truth, be sensitive to the feelings of those involved: reviews should never become witch-hunts.

Once you have a good understanding of how everything worked, make sure that you act on your findings. Project learning is done for a purpose – to improve performance on future projects. Don't keep useful information and ideas to yourself – pass them on to where they can make a difference.

# Holding a project review

**PLAN AHEAD**
Set a date for the review meeting when you are planning the implementation of the project – this should make it easier to get the time in people's diaries.

A "lessons learnt" review meeting is your opportunity to get the team together and discuss how the project went. Hold the meeting as soon as implementation is complete – you can always call a second one, if necessary, once the project has bedded in. Far from duplicating effort, you will find that you actually save time using this approach, because memories are clearer and conclusions are reached more quickly.

Involve as many stakeholders as is practical in this meeting. A process review should take account of the views of everyone involved, within the constraints of cost, time, and availability. If possible, include the views of the client and end user, although in commercial projects, you may need to think carefully about how you are going to get these.

Be clear on what you want to achieve and have an agenda for the meeting. A review meeting can become unfocused and descend into generalizations unless there are specific items to discuss. If you have held interim learning reviews, use the notes from these as a structure. If not, then the PID, plan, and risk log can be a good basis for discussion.

## ❓ ASK YOURSELF... WHAT CAN WE LEARN FROM THIS PROJECT?

- How good was our original scope?
- How accurate were the time and cost estimates?
- Did we have the right mix of people on our team?
- How effectively did the stakeholders work together?
- Where might we have anticipated risks better?
- How effectively did the technology we used perform?
- How well did our project methodology work?
- What project documents were most useful? Which, if any, were missing?

# Documenting your review

Brevity is often the key to a successful project review document, so record the recommendations that you generate following the "lessons learnt" review meeting succinctly. Aim for three key learning points clearly described so that anyone encountering a similar problem in the future can implement your recommendations. If you have to write more because the project was large and complex, structure the document in a way that enables people to gain an overview quickly and then select only the detail that is relevant to them. It can be useful to generate a main document that you distribute to all stakeholders – containing a limited number of key recommendations for the conduct of future projects – and a number of annexes. These can either cover each recommendation in detail or provide more detailed feedback to specific individuals or departments.

Discuss your recommendations with the sponsor. Even if the sponsor does not want to be fully involved in the review process, at the very least you should discuss the findings with him or her before disseminating them to a wider audience.

**THINK SMALL**

Don't underestimate the value of small, easily implemented improvements to your approach. A "lessons learnt" review should identify several of these, and their combined effect can be significant.

# Giving personal feedback

The review phase of your project should also look at the performance of individual members of your team. Although you should have been giving regular feedback throughout the project, people appreciate a final review once it is completed, especially when they've put a lot of effort into making a project successful. You will find that the best workers use feedback from project reviews as a way to build their CV or gather testimonials. Equally, people will be more likely to make a second effort if they know that failure will be investigated and recorded.

# Index

# Acknowledgements

### Author's acknowledgements

My thanks to the many colleagues who have contributed to the success of the Hobbs Partnership as a centre of training and coaching excellence, in particular to Denise Taylorson whose professionalism has been an inspiration and whose support and encouragement I value beyond words. Thanks too to the many world-class clients whose assignments have sharpened my interest and deepened my understanding of project management in the real world. Last, but not least, my thanks to Peter Jones, Kati Dye, and the other talented designers and editors who have transformed my words into a book I am proud to be associated with.

This book is dedicated to Sarah, Alice, Susie, Richard, Fred, and Georgina. God has blessed me greatly through you all.

### Publisher's acknowledgements

The publisher would like to thank Hilary Bird for indexing, Judy Barratt for proofreading, and Charles Wills for co-ordinating Americanization.

### Picture credits

The publisher would like to thank the following for their kind permission to reproduce their photographs:

1 iStockphoto.com: Robert Hadfield; 4–5 iStockphoto.com: Alexandr Tovstenko; 11 Alamy Images: FoodPhotography Eising/Bon Appetit; 17 iStockphoto.com: Vasiliki Varvaki; 20–21 Alamy Images: Redmond Durrell; 24–25 iStockphoto.com: Dmitry Kutlayev; 29 iStockphoto.com: Igor Smichkov; 30–31 Alamy Images: Tim Graham; 32–35 iStockphoto.com: Julien Grondin; 37 iStockphoto.com: Florea Marius Catalin; 43 Corbis: Leo Mason; 46 Getty images: Michael Dunning; 52–53 iStockphoto.com: Emrah Turudu; 57 Alamy Images: Lenscap; 61 iStockphoto.com: Christian Pound; 64–65 iStockphoto.com: Chan Pak Kei; 66 iStockphoto.com: Kanstantsin Shcharbinski.

Every effort has been made to trace the copyright holders. The publisher apologizes for any unintentional omission and would be pleased, in such cases, to place an acknowledgement in future editions of this book.